One cold and quiet Christmas Eve,
The moon was full and bright.
And Peter wondered to himself,
"Will Santa come tonight?"

The other children were asleep,
Tucked warmly in their beds.
And merry dreams of Christmas presents
Danced inside their heads.

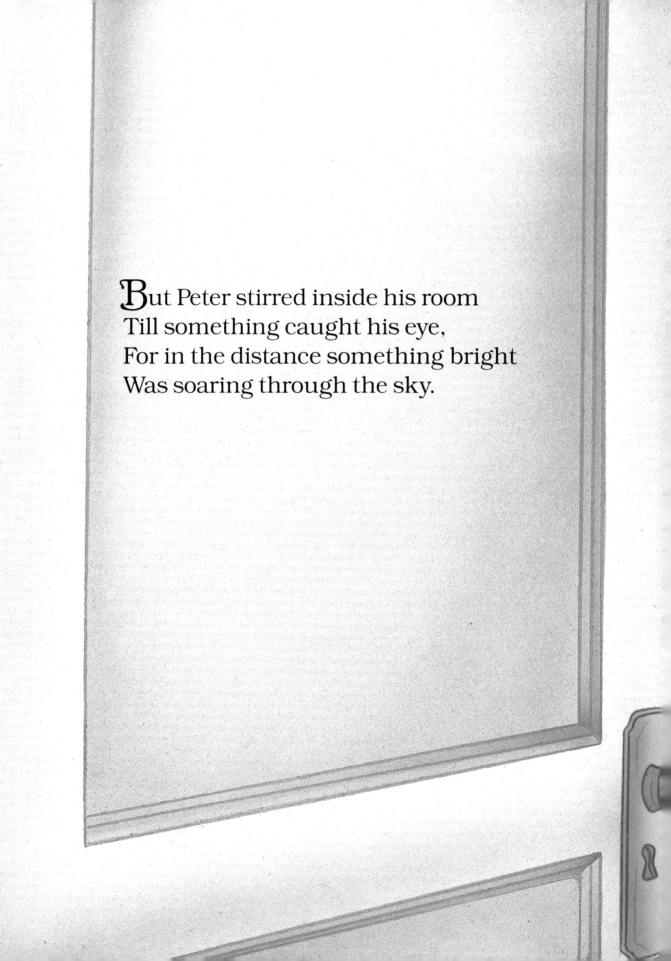

But Peter stirred inside his room
Till something caught his eye,
For in the distance something bright
Was soaring through the sky.

It was Santa racing off
With presents in his sleigh.
He ordered to his reindeer,
"Hurry! Let's be on our way!"

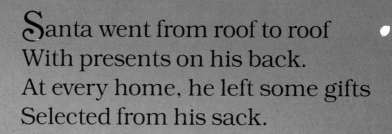

Santa went from roof to roof
With presents on his back.
At every home, he left some gifts
Selected from his sack.

Peter almost gave up hope
That Santa would arrive.
But tapping noises on the roof,
Made Peter come alive.

He hurried down the staircase
And he hid behind the tree.
Was it Santa he had heard?
He had to wait and see.

Soon Santa was inside the room,
Arranging Christmas gifts.
And Peter knew that he'd received
His greatest Christmas wish.